To Ilana:

next you
into your God given
creative side.
I love you always
+ forever -
no matter
what! mom

Closer

Spiritual Reflections for Writers & Thinkers

Molly Ovenden

Molly Ovenden Creativity, LLC

DEDICATION

G od, this book is for You. A labor of love. An exercise in faith. A step closer toward You.

To all women and men from every walk of life who've ever walked on this earth no matter what their background or geographic location is, this book is for you. I pray you'd feel God's love wrapping you up.

To all who hear, hear this; to all who see, see this: be blessed, for you are loved by the Most High God.

AMEN.

Scan this QR code and head on over to grab a copy of your free Questions for Reflection journal pages to help you write, reflect, and think while you read this book.

CONTENTS

ACKNOWLEDGEMENTS

F irst, thank You LORD, for allowing me this opportunity to do something I love: write.

Second, thank you to my dear sweet husband, Max; you are so kind and patient to accept me in all of my creative mess; thank you for all of your encouragement.

Third, thank you to the many people who have continually asked me about this book to hold me accountable. There are so many of you.

Fourth, thank you to my mom and best friend, Maggie Cedarberg; I thank God for you and how you always lift me up and encourage me; listen to me process loads of ideas and possibilities; listen to what I've written no matter what stage it is; and thank you for encouraging me from the beginning of my life to read and write and do so many creative things. Thank you. You are my favorite, Mumsies.

Fifth, thank you to my editors, Mark and Diana Betzold. As you know, I have so many words to say. You stepped in when I needed your support. With patient wisdom and kindness you've helped me persevere with courage and to be who I want to be as a writer, finishing strong.

Last, but not least, thank you to Susie Larson who took me by the hand, prayed for me, and looked me square in the eyes, first in person, then in pixels at the 2019 and 2020 Northwestern Christian Writers Conference. You told me I could get my book into the world. Thank you for leading with such courage and resilient faith.

INTRODUCTION

Hello Lovely Reader,

Thank you tremendously for picking up a copy of this book. I genuinely believe God will touch your heart, for I've had you all in mind from the time I began writing this book.

A couple of notes on the title, *Closer: Spiritual Reflections for Writers and Thinkers.* Faith is important to me, and if it's important to you, too, then we share this desire to grow closer to God. If faith isn't important to you in this season, you're also very welcome to join in. I'm so glad you're here. This book is a place for me to share some of my story with you, offer an opportunity to realize you're not alone in your life, and allow you space to reflect on what I've shared and how it might apply to your life. As a writer and thinker myself, I have lots of words—always! I hope you may be inspired by my stories to reflect and write some of your own, with God's help.

Throughout the book, I use a variety of characteristics of God as names for Him. I relate to God in a variety of ways. He is my Friend, Savior, LORD, King, Lover of my soul and so much more. Because of who God is I long to be closer to Him.

I wanted to take this collection of spiritual reflections a step further than some books I've encountered (and thoroughly enjoyed!) and try to encourage you not only in your faith journey, but in your own writing journey, too. Within the pages of *Closer: Spiritual Reflections for Writers and Thinkers,* you will find short readings with scripture, prayers, and questions to encourage and empower you to reflect on your personal life and challenge you to grow in your faith and relationship with God, and help you write your story with Him as you grow and transform into the writer and person you're made to be.

Additionally, I've provided journaling pages with writing prompts to allow you space to write your responses to the questions, take notes, doodle, write your own prayers to God, or begin to write your own life story of growing closer to God.

With regard to the writing prompts, I encourage you to try setting your timer for 10 minutes to respond to a prompt. In my experience working with individuals who desire to be writers, this increment of time is achievable and allows the opportunity for writers to be effective in getting ideas out at a good pace, while practicing overcoming their inner critic.

I've written this book in a way that gives you a glimpse into my life—a real woman desiring to follow a real God: Jesus Christ. God has spoken to me on many occasions about things in my life, teaching and touching me through everyday situations and objects I encounter. Each time I've written something new, reread, or rewritten something, these same stories I've already experienced have been used by God again and again to help me personally grow even more.

Now, my plan in writing this is that you'll read one each day over the course of 30 days, but I also have in mind that you may forget some days or that you may simply add my book to your collection of many devotionals and it'll be among the possible choices for any given day's devotional time.

At any rate, I am excited you've got this book in your possession. May God continue to bless you richly today and throughout your journey through this book. May He soften your heart to receive more of His love for you personally. May you wake up to the reality of the transformational impact God's love has today in your life. And may you ultimately be encouraged and empowered to rise up and do what you know God has called you to do in Jesus' name. AMEN.

Happy writing!

Molly x

P.S. A Note About the Cover

P.S. Wait! There's one more thing I have to say before it all starts.

I want to share a note about why coin-operated cityscape binoculars are the featured image for the cover of *Closer*.

Why binoculars?

I realize they may not be your first thought when considering a book about spiritual things or writing.

They weren't my first idea either, that's for sure!

I began with close-up photographs of my abstract art, wanting to draw the viewer closer to the texture and color. It just didn't feel right. I didn't know what didn't feel right though.

I want to pause here to specifically thank my graphic design friends, Anthony Schaefer and Andrea Bryant, who gave me tremendous insight. Both were generous with their time answering my questions to empower me while I created the cover. And, they also give me confidence to understand why certain aspects of the design worked well or not. Their support lifted a weight from my shoulders and I'm grateful to have learned a lot from them.

I moved away from using my own art and began a quest for a photograph to communicate the fluidly intangible spiritual content with the heart of the journey (both spiritually getting closer to God and intellectually thinking and writing to get closer to becoming the writer the reader longs to be).

I found a lot of awesome photographs. There are so many talented people in the world!

A lighthouse evoked a sense of showing the way, illuminating ideas, guiding away from danger, and pointing to safety. I don't think *Closer* has all of the answers, but I want it to help you get closer to your destination not just show you where to look or where to avoid.

A fountain pen emphasized the writing aspect over the spiritual and felt too restrictive since *Closer* is a book including writing, but not exactly about writing. Writing is a tool for the journey and the writing craft is not the primary objective of this book, so this wasn't quite right.

A set of binoculars, however, is an interactive object with a shared experience. People from various backgrounds have used the same binoculars to look out over a city, across the ocean, or miles away over mountainside treetops. Many of the coin-operated binoculars I found have a bright red circle in the middle that says, "Turn to clear vision."

My choice to use the binoculars is partly to encompass that sensation of shared experience you and I have as author and reader. Viewing the distance through these lenses requires something from the viewer: an investment and an action. You, my lovely reader have made a financial and time investment to purchase this book and to take time to read and engage with it. It is my hope that with each page you turn your vision would become clearer.

As you look through binoculars you can see what's far away come closer to you. But when you take your gaze away from looking through their lenses, objects are small and far away. Looking through the binoculars shows you where you want to go and brings you visually closer to your destination. They show you the general path to travel to be able to arrive at your destination.

As you set out on the journey, there may be a handful of lookout points with binoculars to help guide you. When we aren't looking for God, He may feel really far away. When we focus on something in the distance, it becomes clearer.

I hope this book brings you clarity as you write and think. And I hope it's one of the tools set along the way, drawing you closer to God on your meandering adventure of life.

FOREWORD

I pray that this book will be an encouragement to you. Molly's example of reflecting on the realities of life, and her challenge to give voice to our thoughts and experiences is refreshingly honest and encouraging. I've known Molly for more than a few years now, and I've seen her own personal vision and creativity continue to develop as she's leaned into these practices.

As you follow the design Molly has laid out, you'll begin to see more clearly how God is able to speak to you through some of the simplest parts of daily life. You'll be encouraged towards deeper reflection about how God actually wants to be involved in the most average and mundane parts of life. You'll experience praying along with Molly as she applies what she's learned to her own life. And you'll be encouraged along your own creative writing journey.

With this book in hand, embracing this regular rhythm will make for a well-grounded and imaginatively encouraging time with God each day, and set the stage for your continued growth as a writer.

Michael Gatlin
Senior Pastor at the Vineyard Church
Duluth, Minnesota

1

ON DREAMING

I think. I dream. In fact, most of my life I have spent dreaming. Once, in Paris I saw the magnificent nude: The Thinker. Often I believe myself to be like him—sitting in contemplative silence, continually pondering, watching the world go by and processing it all. The thing with this possibly brilliant man is that he only watches the world go by. He has bicycles leaning against his naked body and is pooped on by the over-flying bird.

Deep in thought, so focused, I admire his continued thinking—undisturbed by the outside world, but here's my trouble with him. He is unmoved. He is undisturbed by the life passing beyond his posture. Oh, no! How often have I, or do I, just let things happen around and to me? Does the Thinker wish to do something about all the garbage around him? Or does he just take things how they come, never or rarely moving to be the change he actually desires to see?

I want to be the change. I don't want to be passive-aggressively grumbling with irritation, while unwilling to first change my own behavior. If I am going to spend my life thinking about the world around me, and dreaming about how it could be, I'd like to actually do something. However scary it is to make the first move, I want that something to be standing upright to face the world, to wake it up with ripples of action!

This makes me think of the time when Jesus stormed into the temple with a whip and righteous anger, consumed with a zeal for His Father's house, and rebuked all of the people who had made a holy place into a marketplace taking advantage of the poor who'd come to worship. How easily could He have walked past and just ignored it or just said His Father would take care of it.

But He couldn't—He didn't walk past because He was filled with His Father's love and moved by compassion and love toward anger and pain because of these people, well, because of us and how we are unmoved and bringing not the light or hope or peace or life to the areas around us in our spheres of influence.

Jesus does not tell us to sit around and think about all the people in the nations and how it might be possible or even pretty cool to see something happen...but He told me, and He's telling you to GO! and to MAKE! It's not an option and it's not just a nice little thing to think about, it is a command from God, the Creator of the universe!

19 Therefore go and make disciples of all nations, baptizing them in the name of the Father and of the Son and of the Holy Spirit,

Matthew 28:19

Prayer

LORD, You have put it on my heart to care about certain things and this is good. Show me practical ways I can have an impact to glorify Your name in this world today right where I am. Change my heart so I want to take action. Help me to be bold and stand up for Your name, for justice, for love, for truth, for life. LORD, put people in my life who are like-minded so we can encourage each other to stand up and move as You call us to do. Thank You for hearing my prayer. In Jesus' name. AMEN.

· • ● ● ● · ● ● • • ·

Questions for Reflection

What consumes your thoughts? What do you dream about? Ask God if it pleases Him for you to think about it?

What would you like to do? How might God be inviting you to respond or move into action?

Ask God for help with the practical details: What is one step you could take today? One for this week? One for this month? One for this year?

What barriers, roadblocks, areas of sin do you need to confess to God and receive His forgiveness for before you can move forward? List these barriers, then release them to God's control and receive His forgiveness and love in your heart. Then, move on. No, you don't need to forget—you won't get amnesia, but when you receive forgiveness from Jesus and move on, you open up a space for God to work and for Him to bring healing and restoration and ultimately to give you boldness to do what He's calling you to do.

· • ● ● ● · ● ● • • ·

Writing Prompt

Imagine an obstacle as a physical object in your path. Write about an imaginative way to overcome it, as though you were a small child.

Notes

2

ON FATHERS

I sat near a cafe window as I saw what seemed to be a clown car pull up and begin to unload. A petite blond young woman in a yellow coat pulled out a car seat with a sweet little baby in it. Another little body hopped out with her. Meanwhile, yet another child walked around the front of their van. The blond woman closed her door and began walking to enter the building from where I watched. A man then appeared around the same van with a toddler in his arms. Here was this man, a child in his arms, his gaze set upon the parade of his children and his wife before him.

Does his heart well up with love and with pride for his family and for what God has given him? Does he consider what a tremendous gift, authority, and responsibility he has before him? Maybe he does, or maybe he doesn't, but the truth is our perfect heavenly Father cares for us unconditionally and He wants so deeply for us to be affected by His love and caring for us.

I know what it's like to have a cracked and faded picture of a father. Sitting in my dad's lap conjures up a couple pleasant images. For a time, I mostly had memories of absence, hurt, and anger.

I've had people pray for me that the spirit of abandonment would flee from me and I experienced much peace and healing afterward. I was surprised. I didn't realize I felt abandoned. But since my dad passed away when I was 17, unfortunately these negative concepts I have had about fathers are not a rarity.

One message I've heard is that God wants us, His children to perceive Him as our Father—He sent His SON! Because of this, our enemy found this trait, this aspect of our God to be the greatest to destroy in each of our perceptions of and relationships with God. This is the source that makes perfect sense for our negative pictures of God as our Father.

The bottom line is this: Even if you have an amazing dad on earth, your Dad, Creator of everything, is so far superior to even what you could ask, imagine, or dream up. The Father God is in a league of His own when it comes to Fatherhood.

14 For those who are led by the Spirit of God are the children of God. **15** The Spirit you received does not make you slaves, so that you live in fear again; rather, the Spirit you received brought about your adoption to sonship.[a] And by him we cry, *"Abba,*[b] Father." **16** The Spirit himself testifies with our spirit that we are God's children. **17** Now if we are children, then we are heirs—heirs of God and co-heirs with Christ, if indeed we share in his sufferings in order that we may also share in his glory.

Romans 8:14-17

Prayer

Father God, thank You that You have specifically chosen me to call Your own. Help me to fully understand what it means to be Your kid. God, I set down my pride, my hurt, my anger, my apprehension, and my misunderstandings about who we are to each other, and anything else preventing me from hopping up into Your loving and caring arms. Reveal to me my false concept of You from how I've been hurt by my own imperfect human father and father figures. Fix my relationship with You so I can be with You as Your kid and know You as my perfect Father. Thank You, LORD, my Father in heaven for Your gentle faithfulness. In Jesus' name. AMEN.

• • • ● ● • ● ● • • •

Questions for Reflection

What is or was your relationship like with your earthly father?

How has your relationship with your dad helped or hindered you in your relationship with your perfect Heavenly Father in heaven? Ask God to show Himself to you in a fatherly way.

What is your idea of a perfect day with your perfect father? I want to encourage you to actually carry out this perfect day with your heavenly father. You may feel a bit silly because to others you appear to be alone, but you know the truth and it is worth it. If you aren't sure what you want, ask God to show you what you'd enjoy.

• • • ● ● • ● ● • • •

Writing Prompt

Write about a precious memory you have of spending time with your dad.

Notes

3

ON POMEGRANATES

O ne day I saw pomegranates, a favorite of mine, were on sale, so I bought one. I had to ask my mom if she knew how to correctly cut one up. She said no. So, I did the next best thing: I looked it up on the internet.

After skimming through several sites, I felt like I knew what to do:

1. Slice the crown end off to reveal the white flesh and possibly a few edgeling ruby jewels.
2. From the crown end, cut it into almost wedges. It should still be attached at the opposite end, but open up like a wide blossom revealing more sweet pouches.
3. Insert the pomegranate blossom down, having opened it up wide-ish, into a bowl of ice water.
4. Leave it in the ice water for about 15 minutes. The juicy seeds will fall to the bottom of the bowl and any flesh will float on the top.
5. Begin the gentle excavation of the crimson gold nuggets.
6. Break up each wedge and once all seeds are removed, throw the flesh and rind away.
7. Drain the water from the ruby seeds by pouring the contents of the bowl into a fine colander. Be sure to eat a few of the luxurious jewels to test them for quality.

With this new process learned and completed, I added them to a fruit salad I had prepared for a dinner party. They were a perfect final touch and the fruit salad was a hit with those who ate it—all but one. I was so disappointed when I found someone's bowl that had only the expensive and precious, painstakingly prepared pomegranate seeds left.

I sighed, tossed them into the garbage and continued with the clean up and dishwashing. I said to myself, "They just don't know what they're missing."

Over the next few days as I was studying in James and in Proverbs about wisdom, I realized that to me, these pomegranates are like wisdom. The seeds are terribly healthy and are refreshingly satisfying, if only you take time and are willing to prepare the environment to use the seeds, to harvest them, and then to figure out how to make them or it (wisdom), work for you.

Well, you see, wisdom really is like that. God says to ask for wisdom and He'll give it in abundance. Proverbs 2:6 says,

> **6** For the Lord gives wisdom;

> from his mouth come knowledge and understanding.

I like pomegranates and have been praying to be healthy. Seeking knowledge and wisdom as treasure or gold takes effort and time. A person needs to make a time commitment, be patiently persistence, willing to receive the found gift and actually follow through with it.

Seeking knowledge and wisdom like it's golden treasure is similar to my pursuit of healthy fruit. Being able to eat the pomegranate seeds required some learning and patience on my part, like wisdom. And in both circumstances, the result has always been worth the wait.

I had to take ownership of my own search both for healthy things and for wisdom. While I was thrilled by my search and findings of the pomegranate seeds, some were left to waste. Wisdom is like that, too. You or I may be super excited about something God has revealed to us, but while we may be called to share our fruit, others may not be ready to eat it and we have to be okay with that and not be discouraged. Know what you have gained. Seek wisdom.

· • ● ◉ ● • ● ● ● • ·

17 But the wisdom that comes from heaven is first of all pure; then peace-loving, considerate, submissive, full of mercy and good fruit, impartial and sincere.

James 3:17

Prayer

Lord, I want to know You more. I want to be counted as wise in Your sight. I want to follow You to gain wisdom because Your Word says wisdom brings long life. I want to have a long and abundant life serving and living for You. Change my heart to seek You, so I may bear Your good fruit of wisdom and knowledge. Help me to seek wisdom, and then to liberally share this wisdom no matter what others' responses are. Help me to be resilient for You. Thank You, LORD. I trust You. From now on, I will seek wisdom in Jesus' name. AMEN.

Questions for Reflection

In your own words, what is wisdom?

Ask God for ideas about how you can seek wisdom.

Think about the people in your life. Ask God to highlight the wise among them. What character traits does this person have that you see as being wise?

What steps or changes might you make to turn your path toward a life seeking and finding wisdom? If you aren't sure, take a moment to ask God to tell you.

Consider writing a note or setting up a meeting with a person you named in the previous question to ask them about their lives and for advice about how to be wise and pursue wisdom.

• • • ● ● • ● ● • • •

Writing Prompt

Write about a timely conversation you had with a teacher or mentor from your childhood and how it impacted your life.

Notes

4

ON CLEANING THE TOILET

Not my favorite job to do. I do clean, so don't worry if you ever come over to visit. One friend invited me over to her house, but apologized for the state of her toilet, explaining that it's all mildewy because of something in the city's water. I said I didn't mind since mine sometimes looked like that. Basically, I wanted her to get out of the bathroom, so I could relieve my poor bladder.

She continued on however, saying she wanted to use one of those bleach tablets that turns the water blue for many flushes, but she didn't think it looked good, that it was like a college dorm room of guys.

"Thank you for showing me where the bathroom is," and I gently closed the door before she would think of more problems than mildew in the bathroom.

While it is a disgusting, laborious process to clean the toilet bowl with a scrub brush and disinfectant, wipe a cloth over the tank cover, handle, outside of the tank, top and bottom of the lid, top and bottom of the seat, outside of the bowl and the hose part that connects to the floor; it has to be done.

Toilet cleaning requires some endurance. The result, however, is very pleasant, satisfying, and relieving, knowing this clean smell means a fresh perspective at least for the day.

I heard somewhere about a lady who had OCD to the extent that if she ever had parties, she patrolled her bathroom and would clean it after every use, which included replacing the flower petals in the toilet water, to make it look so clean and fresh. Yikes! While using the toilet at her house would be lovely and quite a luxurious event, in a way, I don't think I'll ever do that at my house.

When I think about it, the ultimate toilet cleaner is really God. As horrible as we think the scum and gunk in the toilet is, the sin harboring in our hearts and minds that keeps us from connecting with God, is so far worse, rank and gross!

God is actually willing to clean the scum from our hearts. He wants to. He made the ultimate sacrifice of His own Son so He could clean up the messes in our hearts. While God does not have OCD, He asks that we allow Him to practice what we may see as His cleansing tendencies: He wants us to be willing to open the toilets of our hearts to be cleansed after each use by the Ultimate Toilet Cleaner.

If we allow Him in, we'll be in pretty good shape. While that flower woman has some difficulties enjoying a party and her guests, at least her toilet is clean and fresh—perpetually!—similar to the bleach tablet that turns the water blue.

What if we had gauges on ourselves to determine whether or not your heart or my heart was in need of some cleaning? Like, what if the water of our hearts would go from brilliant blue to lighter and lighter until it's back to clear and starting to get scummy? What if we had God bleach tablets in our hearts?

What if we were willing to open up and let our all-amazing loving God clean us out—swill out, flush out any muck that's come into our hearts recently—since whenever the last flush was? How would our lives be changed?

• • ● ● ● • ● ● ● • •

10

Create in me a pure heart, O God,

and renew a steadfast spirit within me.

Psalm 51:10

Prayer

LORD, come close and clear out all the ick in my life. I admit all the places where I've done wrong and offended You right now. I am sorry and I want to live a life that is pleasing to You. Clear out the junk in my life so love can flow easily out of me and help people turn to You to glorify You, LORD. Remind me to continually clear out my heart's muck and residue from the world and my own sinfulness. I want You to clean me up. Make me fresh and whole and new. Thank You, LORD, for Your grace and persistence. In Jesus' name. Amen.

Questions for Reflection

What are some routine activities you daily or weekly or monthly take part in?

How regularly do you take part in asking God to clear out your heart? How often do you confess your sins to God and actively receive His forgiveness?

What do you need God to cleanse you of right now? Write it down and then talk to Him, asking Him to renew you into the person He has in mind for you to be.

What ways do you think you can make your routine cleaning activities coincide with your routine heart cleaning prayers?

• • • ● ● • ● ● • •

Writing Prompt

Make a list of the regular tasks you've done over the last 24 hours. Choose one and write about it using specific details and all five senses.

Notes

5

On Gardening

I remember meeting a lady who said she'd gone a bit overboard on her gardening ventures. She zealously planted 40 tomato plants, among other things, also in abundance. She said even though the tomato season was poor the past year, she still had way more than she could handle.

I want her problem. I don't have a green thumb. I dream of having a massive garden I can cultivate—that I can preserve by canning the produce and making into pies—sweet and savory, that I can freeze, and that I can trade for other more expensive things, which would allow me to physically provide for our family as my full time job. Wouldn't that be cool?

If I ever feel overworked, then I should ask for help—ask my neighbors to spend an hour or two to help me work the soil, plant, pull weeds, harvest a crop, and then they could also reap the benefits I have sown, which they too, put a few beads of sweat into. I think this lady could have dealt with asking for help to reap a better harvest. I wish I would've known her before and that she would have asked me to help her—I would have loved it.

There is definitely something about a partnership and teamwork. Another friend of mine told me about one evening she'd had a party and ended up feeling so alone because she'd not asked anyone for help, and then she ended up doing a lot of the cleanup herself. God said that in the beginning he found it was not good for man to be alone, so he made Eve as a helper for Adam, so they could be in community. There's an old saying: "many hands make light work."

When it comes to helping out and doing work, I oftentimes think we are unaware of a need for help. I didn't know about this woman's gardening endeavors, or my friend's feelings of abandonment. In regard to kingdom work with God, a lot of us are in the dark, not knowing, or maybe we're lethargic about it.

But we really have no excuse as followers of Jesus Christ. He says we've got to pray for people to wake up and mobilize into action to harvest for the kingdom. You and I are workers and one of our jobs is to ask God for more willing laborers like us to do His will.

The harvest is ready and the workers are few—let's get some people to help us live a good life by harvesting all the blessings..

• • ● ● ● • ● ● ● • •

37 Then he said to his disciples, "The harvest is plentiful but the workers are few. **38** Ask the Lord of the harvest, therefore, to send out workers into his harvest field."

Matthew 9: 37-38

• • ● ● ● • ● ● ● • •

Prayer

LORD, thank You that I am answering Your call to do Your will. Please empower me to do Your will. Increase the desire and urgency in my heart to pray that many would come to know You. Help me to be faithful to You and show me how to encourage others who love You to rise up and also be praying. Help me to be more like You, having compassion toward those who don't know You yet. Help me to be willing. Thank You for the privilege and honor to serve Your kingdom in Jesus' name. AMEN.

• • • ● ● • ● ● • •

Questions for Reflection

Why do you think the harvest is plentiful but lacking workers?

Where do you see yourself in these verses? Are you part of the harvest or are you a worker doing the harvesting?

Ask God to show you what it looks like for you to work in the harvest field? What is your everyday harvest field? (e.g., work, school, neighborhood, communities, etc.)

When can you set aside a regular time to obey Jesus' command to pray for the Lord of the harvest to send out workers into his harvest field? How about right now? Now, I agree it may feel a little silly to actually pray those words, but I know praying words from the Bible is powerful and I encourage you to pray verses regularly.

• • • ● ● • ● ● • •

Writing Prompt

Write about a time you visited a farm. What did you see? What did you learn?

Notes

Thank you so much for reading my book! What do you think so far?

I really appreciate all of your feedback and I love hearing what you have to say.

Here's the thing: I need your input to make my future books even better.

Please take two minutes now to leave a helpful review online to let me know what you thought of the book.

Scan this code to bring you to the review site.

Thanks so much! :)

Happy reading!

Molly

6

On Water

Think of a time you've played in water outside. You probably splashed, glided, danced, floated, jumped, waded, but when you stopped, the water around you settled and became calm.

Did you see reflections peering just off the surface of the lake or gentle stream or was it such a mad rushing that only the gurgling, foaming edges were still enough to hold your reflection? If then there was a disruption in the stillness to move your watery portrait, did you think of one of those silly dream or memory sequences on TV or in a film when the picture goes wobbly as the character's mind takes over?

Our own physical reflection causes us to look back on what's happened to bring us where we are in life, with regard to our relationships, careers, schools, ideas about God, daily habits, dreams or aspirations. We also are sometimes rippled forward, imagining the future. What do we want to do differently in the future? The same? What dreams do we perceive or desire for ourselves? How do we think we may have these things come to fruition? Look at yourself in the mirror, watery or otherwise, and consider who you are today, who you used to be, and who you are to become.

My prayer for us today is that we would be still for long enough to feel confident about who God's created us to be. I pray that we'd smile at our reflection in the mirror, that we'd have the assurance we are beautiful and chosen people, called upon by God to do great and unimaginable things. May we rest in the truth that through God we are made perfect and whole and capable to do what He calls us to do. With God, we are good enough.

May we meet our own gaze and speak in an encouraging and empowering way to ourselves. "[Insert your name here], you are beautiful, fearfully and wonderfully made, darn good looking actually, and you are made by God to do gigantic things. He makes you strong to do them. You are confident in who you are and you know whose you are. Stand up tall and smile today because this is the day of the LORD: rejoice and be glad in it!" Now, get a move on doing what God is putting on your heart to do, knowing His reflection is more accurate and more important than yours.

11

Let the king be enthralled by your beauty;

honor him, for he is your lord.

Psalm 45:11

Prayer

LORD, please help me to see myself as You see me: that I am beautiful, that I am purified and set apart because of Jesus on the cross and rising again, that I am capable and a co-heir with Christ, that I am strong with You and more than a conqueror, and that I am Your own child You chose and adopted into Your life. Help me to understand how You've brought me out of darkness and how You'd like me to shine Your light, life and truth in the future. Help me to take my focus off myself and turn it to You: A constant vision of steady strength, the way, the truth, the life, purity, grandeur, glory, love.

• • • ● ● • ● ● • • •

Questions for Reflection

Who does God say You are? You may want to have this be an on-going response. Leave a space to write in verses that answer this question any time you read the Bible. Ask God to help you hear more of what He says about you.

What do you think God wants you to do? What is your calling? Spend a few minutes asking God and waiting for a response. Even if you are sure, take a moment to be still before the LORD and wait for an answer, clarification or direction.

List three steps you can take right now, this week and this month toward your calling. Now do your first step, remembering God is on your side, loves you unconditionally for who you are, and thinks highly of you.

• • • ● ● • ● ● • • •

Writing Prompt

Write about the most beautiful waterscape you've seen.

Notes

ON TIMERS

S itting by myself at my favorite teashop, I watched the sand passing through the timer. In a sort of dazed, reflective mood, I wanted to drink my relaxing cup of tea. It seemed like it was taking forever for it to finish steeping. Actually, it almost seemed like nothing was even moving at all in the timer. I leaned in and took a closer look. Wow! Upon closer examination, bajillions of tiny granules passed through the timer—really quickly even!

From far away, it didn't appear anything was happening but the obvious passing of time. The sand from far away did not seem to pile up or to even decrease from the upper bulb. At this time, I was actually waiting for my visa to come through so I could return to England to become Max's wife. I wanted to be there, yet I had to wait when life seemed to move at a painfully slow pace.

At another critical point of waiting, a friend saw a picture of an hourglass (not knowing anything about this story of mine) with the same concept of it appearing to be broken with no time passing, but instead, the time was standing still. I felt like God was reminding me it would be good to realign my perspective. If I could see things from God's perspective I'd understand that in reality, my application form probably wasn't lost, fallen and stuck, wedged between some desk and a wall, forgotten, but that many people had to look at it and fill out paperwork—all things that take time, little movements that seem like nothing.

Each little granule of progress brings me closer to what I'm waiting for: a cup of tea, governmental permission to move, to hear from a manager about a potential job, and so on. My life, and yours, clearly has time passing, but can feel like we're making no progress.

Sometimes we need a change in our perspective. We need to shift our mindset to be closer to God so we can more fully grasp what is actually going on beyond what our eyes perceive.

We can learn to see the bajillions of tiny granules, moments, discoveries, which are all occurring while we wait; and even when we may not always see them, they do, in God's perspective, truly have an impact on the passing of time and on nearing the goal or the end of a waiting time. All of this requires a perspective shift only achieved by God's transformation and grace.

· · • ● ● • ● ● • · ·

4

A thousand years in your sight

are like a day that has just gone by,

or like a watch in the night.

Psalm 90:4

8 But do not forget this one thing, dear friends: With the Lord a day is like a thousand years, and a thousand years are like a day.

2 Peter 3:8

Prayer

LORD, help me to see things how You do. God I want Your perspective on how time passes. Open my eyes to see more of how You see things. LORD, I want to know You more and I want to be the best for You. Help me to honor You with my time and schedule while I am waiting. Help me to see the point and meaning in little tasks and help me to realize there is always a whole lot more going on than I am ever aware of. LORD, I want a shift in my perspective. I want Your kingdom perspective. Thank You, Father, in Jesus' name. Let it be so. AMEN.

Questions for Reflection

What are you waiting for?

Examine your heart. Let God examine it, too. Record your thoughts and emotions during this waiting time.

Is the way you feel honoring and trusting God? If yes, how can you maintain this steadiness? If no, what do you need to do to change? Ask God to help you.

Writing Prompt

Write about a time you had to wait that had surprising results.

Notes

8

ON COLORADO PEACHES

M y mom clasps her hands with wide eyes and a giant smile in anticipation of peach season in the summertime. If you can't wait for them and give in to eating before they're in season, you'll bite into a dry rock. On the other hand, if you wait too long, they will be mushy and rotten.

So, when they are in season, you must take full advantage of them. Buy as many as you can afford and eat them in any way possible: peach pie, cobbler, tart, crumble, with yogurt and granola, sauce; can them, make them into jam...Make the season's crop work for you. Make it as plentiful as you can, and make it stretch by canning or freezing, if possible, and share the wealth if you can manage to!

I also wait for these peaches all year long with my mom. They are so tasty. We wait and we wait, and when they finally come they are always splendidly worth the wait: sweet and juicy as ever!

Sometimes we have something we know God has promised will happen, but we're itching to get to that season. Sometimes we don't know exactly when the peach season is going to be, or it ends up coming a little earlier or later than we expect; the peaches are ready when they're ready—so it is with God's timing.

He is ready when He is ready. If we jump the gun and bite into the outcome or season before it's the right time, we will be disappointed by a dry, flavorless opportunity. If we wait too long, ignoring the Holy Spirit nudges telling us it's the right time, we'll miss the crop, the opportunity God prepared for us—we'll have missed out on what He had for us because we were too busy or forgot or just couldn't get around to taking advantage of the season when the juicy fruit was ready.

But, when we know the timing is right, we'd better be ready to be blown away with oodles of, crates upon crates of sweet juicy blessings. Load up while it's going. Take it all in.

When it comes, it is a blessing you can share—go ahead! Be a blessing to another or many others. Pack in as much of the goodness that you discover and somehow, save any excess for later. Build a memorial to God, showing how He has blessed you when you'd been in such great anticipation. Freeze a memory or verse or moment when God spoke to you during this season. Put some to good use now and preserve some of it for later.

· · • ● ● · ● ● ● · ·

7

Be still before the Lord

and wait patiently for him;

do not fret when people succeed in their ways,

when they carry out their wicked schemes.

Psalm 37:7

• • • ● ● • ● ● • • •

Prayer

LORD, give me the grace to accept Your timing. Keep me from being stubborn, controlling, or jumping in too early. Keep me from being prideful and hardening my heart against Your words. Prevent me from not recognizing Your voice, or missing the opportunity. God, I don't want to miss out on what You have for me. Increase my awareness of how You are at work in my life. Give me new understanding and new eyes to receive in Your timing. Help me be patient and wait for the good stuff: Your absolute best for me. Don't hold back, LORD. And God, while I wait, I want to get to know You more, so I can be ready to receive all You have for me. Thank You. In Jesus' name. AMEN.

• • • ● ● • ● ● • • •

Questions for Reflection

How does it make you feel when you need to wait for God? Describe or think about your current circumstances or a past situation.

How often have you spent time with God just being still at His feet? Consider doing that regularly. What does God have to say about the time you spend with Him?

What promise or answer are you waiting for? Bring it again to God, lay it at His feet, then wait at His feet. Ask him about it. Ask Him to show Himself to you. Spend 5, 10, 15 minutes or more at His feet. When you get up, leave your prayers and anticipation with Him.

• • • ● ● • ● ● • •

Writing Prompt

Write about a family food tradition.

Notes

9

ON BREATHING

P ause for a moment here. Close your eyes, and just breathe. Let go of the frantic feeling of constant doing, doing, doing and simply breathe. Fill your belly deeply and slowly, and then allow the air to inflate your lungs just beyond what is comfortable for you. I've done a bit of yoga and some relaxation exercises which emphasize breathing.

I want to admit I know there is a lot of controversy among Christians surrounding this form of exercise and meditation. I have come across a couple teachers who taught me poses and relaxation methods and muscle control without encouraging me to believe in a different spirituality. I also have been to classes which encouraged students to be one with the earth and be goddesses with all the power in them on their own without God. Students left these classes looking dead and run down, rather than strengthened and refreshed—so I never went to those instructors' classes again. One time, I actually walked out shortly after it'd begun because I felt spiritual heaviness and oppression, so I got out of it as quickly as I could and did a different workout that day.

In yoga there is always a big focus on our breathing: slowly and deeply making each breath count and work for us maximizing our oxygen exchange. This slow, deep, rhythmic breathing brings focus to the time of stretching, balance, and muscle toning. In our time with God, we always need to set everything aside to bring focus to Him. It's okay to hear the whistling through our nostrils and our gurgling, digesting stomachs. It's okay to hear ourselves swallow and to hear our hearts beating. We become still, quiet, aware and the oxygen itself even brings calmness. We feel happy. Breathing is life.

God gives and takes away. He breathes the earth into existence. He gives us breath every moment of every day, and has done so since we were born. Jewish tradition in Biblical times used to pronounce God's name, Yahweh, and say the sound His name makes is like the first inhalation of a newborn just come from the womb and like the final exhalation of a dying body.

There is power and life in a breath and in our LORD. So, don't worry about just simply hanging out with God, being able to hear your own breath as you wait to hear from Him. When you sit and just dwell in His presence, you begin to be open to His full character and His righteousness. He is supremely good and He knows He is worthy to be praised and lifted high. It's good to breathe His life in.

10

He says, "Be still, and know that I am God;

I will be exalted among the nations,

I will be exalted in the earth."

Psalm 46:10

Prayer

LORD, help me to quiet my heart and mind and just be in Your presence. Thank You that You are always with me. Thank You that in the stillness and solitude, with You, I'm never alone. Thank You that there is nothing to be afraid of when I am sitting still in Your presence. Help me lay aside my busy mind and all the distractions so I can meditate on Your law and on Your greatness of character. I love You, my Lord. Let Your will be done. Discipline me into quiet wisdom and strength to follow You. LORD, help me to take in the mighty power of Your sonship. I want to know how to exalt You in the highest. In Jesus' name. AMEN.

• • • ● ● • ● ● ● • ·

Questions for Reflection

What distractions do you encounter whenever you come to spend time with God? What prevents you sometimes from even beginning to spend time with Him?

Ask God how you might minimize or eliminate these distractions?

What do you want most when you go into a time with God? If you aren't sure, begin the process by asking God to show you your desires.

Who is God to you? List examples from your life of His character and authority.

Writing Prompt

Write about someone's birth or death you witnessed.

Notes

10

On Shooting and Guns

M y brother told me about some of the training he has had to help him learn how to safely and effectively operate and handle a gun. He told me about how he learned of a particular training that happens in the military. When a soldier gets really good, he, the gunman, sits in the room with the target while his teammates shoot past him to hit the target.

How terrifying! But to not be able to trust his friends and fellow soldiers would actually be much more terrifying. Though there is fire and danger all around him, as long as he sits in the designated spot, trusts his fellow soldiers, and does not flee in fear or for any other reason, he will actually be safe.

Psalm 91 says that though disaster may be occurring all around you, no harm will come to you if you walk beside God. In the Chronicles of Narnia, someone asks about Aslan, whether or not he is safe to be around. The response is a resounding "No!" But, he's good, they say. Like God, because of His goodness, it is safe to trust in Him. And like the verse in the Psalms says, bad things may be happening around us that are unsafe.

We may feel like a trusting soldier during target practice. While that soldier may be afraid at first, the more he gets to know his friends and their character, the more he will be able to trust them and feel safe and protected in their presence. It makes sense, then, that if we understand who God is, He can be our best friend. Spending time with Him to know we can fix our gaze on Him no matter what horrible things are happening around us, we are in a good position of protection by God when we focus on Him and trust Him.

That soldier in training can trust his friends and fellow soldiers; even more can we trust God because of His perfect love. He'll never miss the target. We really don't need to worry about His aim being off. His aim is never off.

7

A thousand may fall at your side,

ten thousand at your right hand,

but it will not come near you.

Psalm 91:7

Prayer

Oh, LORD, my Refuge, my Love, my Protector. Thank You that You are good and thank You that I am safe in Your sheltering wings. Praise You that Your track record is flawless and that You are trustworthy. I want a gift of faith. Supernaturally instill within my heart the ability to trust You more. Help me to get to know You more. Reveal Yourself to me, LORD, so I can trust in who You are and who You say I am. Thank You for Your protective and patiently powerful hand upon my life. In Jesus' name. AMEN.

• • • ● ● • ● ● • • •

Questions for Reflection

How well do you trust God with every aspect of your life?

Why do you think you trust Him that much or that little? Ask God what is preventing you from trusting Him more.

What are some of God's attributes you have witnessed, which contribute to understanding how trustworthy God is?

• • • ● ● • ● ● • • •

Writing Prompt

Write about an experience of war.

Notes

11

ON BROCCOLI SUNSHINE

When I lived in the dorms my freshman year at college, I had a meal plan to eat in the dining center—or, "the DC." They served what they called, "almost as good as Mom's cooking" for each meal, and really, it was pretty good. One dish in particular which I grew fond of was Broccoli Sunshine. There was always a handwritten menu board at the entrance so we would know if we wanted to eat there in the DC, or instead order pizza or Chinese to eat in our dorm rooms.

On Broccoli Sunshine days, I was there in the DC! Honey-glazed broccoli with carrots was always really good. It was one way to get us students to eat our vegetables. I have loved broccoli for awhile, but it wasn't always the case. For several years starting when I was a young teenager, I prayed God would change my taste buds so I'd be able to eat more healthily. And He did! I'll eat almost anything now.

Often we try to force kids to eat broccoli. "It's good for you," we say. But they won't eat it. Maybe they'd like peas, carrots, spinach or artichokes—or maybe they would eat Broccoli Sunshine.

I think when we talk to people about God, we should have a Broccoli Sunshine approach: All the good stuff is still there, it's just more approachable. Or maybe we need a whole different approach, like the squash, corn, or brussels sprouts way instead. God made us all with an ingrained understanding and ability to perceive Him, and we will, but in different ways, through different experiences.

I believe we, as disciples, whom Jesus sent out to preach good news to the poor, need to be open and observant to be able to know how to approach people and talk to them about God. It can be so tempting to try to shove the "good news" down somebody's throat because we know it is good for them. Well, when people are treated that way, we know they actually are much less likely to want to know God or be around anyone who is not going to allow them to come to the truth by their own choosing.

8

Taste and see that the Lord is good;

blessed is the one who takes refuge in him.

Psalm 34:8

12 Live such good lives among the pagans that, though they accuse you of doing wrong, they may see your good deeds and glorify God on the day he visits us.

1 Peter 2:12

Prayer

LORD, fill me with Your Holy Spirit: With Your wisdom, truth, grace, discernment, joy and most importantly, Your love! Fill me up to overflowing with Your perfect love and guide me in the ways to encounter people who need to meet You. Help me know how to present Your goodness to them. Give me courage to share my own experience of who You are and how good You are. Give me grace for myself to hear You and compassionate patience for the people You lead me to. Thank You for Your Spirit to direct me and to speak the words you bring to my lips. In Jesus' name, may every eye see how great you are! AMEN.

• • ● ● ● • ● ● • •

Questions for Reflection

How did God finally get hold of your heart? Who did He use to speak to you? What did they do that helped convince you of the truth? What characteristics did this person or these people have that made you more inclined to receive God and their message?

Was there anyone who, well-intentioned or not, made you not want to know God, or someone who called themself a Christian but has steered you away or left a bad taste in your mouth? What characteristics made you want to steer clear? Ask God to help you forgive and let go of any hurt or bitterness you've been holding against them.

Think about people in your sphere of influence (friends, family members, neighbors, co-workers, etc.) who do not yet know Jesus. Make a list of three names. How can you implement good characteristics, like those you listed in the first question, to have a positive impact and lead these people to experience God? Spend time thanking God for the opportunity to work alongside Him. Pray for them to have a life changing experience with God, and then ask Him how you can play a practical role in their lives. It might start out that you are interceding for them; that's not a small task. A person's salvation and spiritual choices are not up to you. It is not our job to convert anyone. That is God's job. Our job is to love people and do good works, so people will see this love and good works and want to glorify the LORD themselves.

• • • ● ● • ● ● • • •

Writing Prompt

Write about someone who inspires your beliefs.

Notes

12

ON EXPLODING DISHES

One time when I was doing what my mom had done successfully many times before to bake bread, we had a bit of an accident. You see, the recipe calls for preheating the oven for 20 minutes at 450 degrees Fahrenheit, or about 230 degrees Celsius, with a baking stone and a tray below to fill with water.

The recipe says to use a metal broiler tray, but my mom said that using a glass baking dish, her favorite blue one, was fine to use since it worked the past few times. This time, then, should not have been any different, but I am quite afraid it was. When I opened the door and quickly tossed in the cup of water, there was a loud bang and shattering.

The dish had exploded all over the inside of the oven and outward onto all of the kitchen floor. I felt so thankful I did not get hurt, and that nobody else was in the kitchen with me. I was so scared by the explosion and was shaken for a few minutes before my mom and her friend and I all cleaned up.

I told mom that maybe next time we will actually follow the directions. The authors of the bread book knew what they were talking about. Like, they see a bigger picture than we do: they are experts. Kind of like God. When God tells us to do something, we must obey.

Obedience is key to following a recipe in our life with God. He has His reasons for telling us to do this or that because He knows more than we do. He's got the bigger picture in mind—He created the bigger picture! We may think we know better, because "it worked last time," to do it a different way from what God's directions are. We must obey Him, no matter what, because He's God: the ultimate author of the recipe for our lives. If we don't obey...it may be explosive!

32

"Now then, my children, listen to me;

blessed are those who keep my ways.

Proverbs 8:32

Prayer

Oh, LORD, You know my true heart. I confess that I sin against You by not doing what I know You tell me to do. Thank You for Jesus who made the way for me to receive forgiveness. I confess my wholehearted trust in You, LORD, and I want to be obedient. Give me grace to do Your will. LORD, I lay down my life before You. Help me to follow Your way and to obey Your commands and callings. Keep me from disobedience that in turn causes harm. I trust You, LORD. Thank You for Your guidance. In Jesus' name. AMEN.

Questions for Reflection

Recount a time God told you to do something and you were disobedient, doing it your own way. What were the consequences?

Remember now a time you were obedient. How were you blessed, even if it was a time when you were unable to see the outcome right away?

Ask God for direction and clarity about areas in life you know He is telling you to obey now? Will you be obedient? Ask Him for help to obey.

• • • ● ● • ● ● • •

Writing Prompt

Write about a time you didn't follow the rules. What were the results?

Notes

13

ON THE MILE RUN

I used to hate running. I'd often dream about it though. "Wouldn't it be cool if I were a runner?!"

Whenever I'd hear somebody talking about the great rush of feel-good feelings that happens after a run, I'd look at them with disbelief and more than a hint of disgust. I just know it was impossible, but I didn't know why they all lied about it.

After dreaming about all the wonders of running, I'd remember how horrible it is to sweat, pant and turn beet red. My best time ever of running one mile was in middle school when it took nine minutes and fifty-six seconds. I worked so hard and really pushed myself on that. I believe I actually ran the whole way, never slowing to a walking speed.

My worst time was in elementary school. I lived close to the school, and on the path where we did the mile, I could see my house across the lake. It was raining hard that day and I was in a rather pitiful state. I even stopped to stare at my house across the lake, willing my mom, who I knew was there, to come paddling across the lake in our canoe to get me, to save me from this wretched rainy day horror that was the mile run. It seemed to take "forever" to 'run' that mile. I think even the kid with bad asthma finished before me.

As a young teen, I was so determined to run well. I wanted to actually finish my four laps around the school track with a time I was proud of myself for. I genuinely pushed myself and it was genuinely awful! I felt sick and overheated and horrible, and I didn't ever want to do it again.

So I promised myself: I will never run a race and I pray I won't ever be pursued!

Amusingly, my school days of despising physical activity are gone and I actually transitioned to loving running. Around 2014, the love of running came to me. At the time of this writing, I've completed numerous 5Ks and 10Ks, and half marathons, and I'm currently training for my third marathon (26.2 miles).

Actually, there is a race I am currently running that isn't requiring me (yet!) to physically run. Paul says we should press on to run the race to finish and win the prize. At least in this race there is a point. There is a reason to be running, one that we may feel happy to physically run, if necessary. There is a goal to press on toward, and there is a prize.

We aren't just running along in life, ponytail bouncing and going nowhere; we are living a good life, bringing glory to God. We are pursuing a great endpoint. That endpoint is actually the beginning of everlasting eternal life with our Maker and Lover, and this race is a worthwhile use of time and energy.

• • ● ● ● • ● ● ● • •

12 Not that I have already obtained all this, or have already arrived at my goal, but I press on to take hold of that for which Christ Jesus took hold of me. **13** Brothers and sisters, I do not consider myself yet to have taken hold of it. But one thing I do: Forgetting what is behind and straining toward what is ahead, **14** I press on toward the goal to win the prize for which God has called me heavenward in Christ Jesus.

Philippians 3:12-14

• • ● ● ● • ● ● ● • •

Prayer

Thank You LORD for giving me spiritual legs to endure all You called me to. LORD, I realize that enduring any race has so much to do with attitude; I want to have an attitude of determination, motivated by the prize of eternal life with You at the end of the race. Help me to be strong and not hold an attitude like that of the seven-year-old, pitying herself in the cold rain, nearly giving up entirely. I want to be strong and I want to race to bring You glory. Help me to do Your will. Help me to finish this race strong and in Jesus' name. AMEN.

• • • • • • • • • • •

Questions for Reflection

What are common daily hurdles that prevent or delay you from running this meaningful good race?

What makes the goal of finishing the race, eternity in heaven with Jesus, worthwhile to you? What do you think heaven will be like?

Ask God to show you your training plan. What steps can you take this week to become more spiritually fit to run this life-giving race?

• • • • • • • • • • •

Writing Prompt

Write about a situation that has required you to persevere and endure till the end.

Notes

14

ON MUD

When I was a little kid, my big brother and I would work on our off-road jeep. We would dream about how cool it would be to modify it, so the exhaust would spit flames. Then we lamented it would no longer be road legal to drive, but it would still be awesome, that's for sure. He taught me how to change the oil and would always explain to me how everything worked. Sadly, I was pretty young, so almost none of this knowledge stuck with me.

But after all of the day's lessons and preparation, we would drive our jeep through mud. Lots of mud. We would drive around slightly bored on the normal highways and roads until we found a big grassy lot-or if we were lucky enough that it rained-an abandoned, muddy lot. We probably weren't supposed to be ripping up these properties. Even though they appeared to be abandoned, they must have been owned by someone.

One rainy afternoon we were really tearing it up down by the river in a rewarding, secluded spot. Laughing and watching all the mud spit up from the massive treads of the tires, we were having a blast! We had windshield wipers going like mad and we bounced along, whipping around in circle after circle—it was so much fun I didn't even get dizzy or carsick!

We had a grand time until the engine roared and the tires spun. They spun round and round in the most slippery of mud: a giant rut. Being the experienced off-road driver my brother was, and I, being taught by him, we both understood he could accelerate as much as he wanted, but we would NEVER get anywhere no matter what, as long as we were stuck in this muddy rut.

Quick thinking had my brother out of the jeep in no time to check out how deep we were in: pretty deep. I was instructed to stay inside; I might have been the next thing stuck! My big brother wandered around in this 'middle of nowhere' to find something to give us some traction to get out and going again.

Several minutes later he came back with a stop sign! He'd found it somewhere in the field. He positioned it expertly beneath the front of the stuck wheels, and holding our breath with a quick hopeful thought, he hit the pedal. We felt stuck and stuck and stuck and....FREE! We roared off. If my brother had not persevered to find something useful to move us forward and to get us out of the rut, we'd still be there! Remember how I said it was abandoned?!

Have you ever felt as though you were, or even right now are, in a muddy rut of a situation, stuck forever? I often have felt like that. I wasn't naturally a persevering, determined kind of kid like my brother was then, so if it had just been me, I'd have stayed stuck in that field.

I very much remember getting a bit worried and depressed back in the jeep, praying we could get out. My spirit was a bit crushed and I was sure life was over then and there. Fortunately, I had someone to help me out of it, my brother. With God, we have help, too. With God, we can persevere and we can be pulled from our sticky situations, too.

• • • ● ● ● • ● ● ● • •

2 Consider it pure joy, my brothers and sisters,[a] whenever you face trials of many kinds, **3** because you know that the testing of your faith produces perseverance. **4** Let perseverance finish its work so that you may be mature and complete, not lacking anything.

James 1:2-4

• • • ● ● • ● ● • • •

Prayer

God, I do want to be mature, and I do want to learn to persevere through the trials and difficult times of ruts and stuckness in my life. God, I want a supernatural gift of faith to trust You and I want the Holy Spirit to empower me with Your grace so I can be strong enough with You to press on and through difficult situations. Help me to see past the trials and see through to the maturity that will come from persevering. Truly LORD, I do not want to lack anything. Thank You for Your faithfulness and for helping me through life to get closer to You. Thank you, in Jesus. AMEN.

• • • ● ● • ● ● • • •

Questions for Reflection

How have you learned to persevere to get unstuck and out of unpleasant, my-life-is-at-its-end situations?

Who are the people in your life who seem resilient and able to push through difficulties? Consider asking them for help and wisdom about how to persevere. They may be able to help you get free from the muddy rut in your life like my brother did for us!

What spiritual rut do you feel yourself in right now? If you aren't in one, praise God! And thank Him! But, if you are, ask God for help and to see what you can be doing to look for the stop sign kind of leverage?

Writing Prompt

Write about a time you were stuck.

Notes

15

ON WEIGHTLIFTING

I've never been very strong. And people never think I look strong either, but I've surprised a couple people by my strength. When I was younger, my family taught me to work really hard. Part of that work took place moving our friends whenever they happened to move to a new house. Even from a young age, I'd carry boxes.

Another time, there was a big storm that caused our friends to lose more than a dozen old trees in their backyard. I picked up the sawed logs and carried and stacked them into piles. While I'm not naturally strong, I've learned to try hard. That has caused a bit of pain for me lifting with my back instead of my legs or arms, although I've continued learning from my younger experiences.

I am strong emotionally. I don't always feel strong, but people tell me I am. I guess, rather than reacting to someone's negative comment, or losing it over a highly stressful situation, sometimes I'm able to keep it together and sometimes I've learned to tough it out. I've learned to pray or talk to a friend to process my feelings.

When my dad died, I was 17 and I think I got tough from that. But I have seen that so-called strength as a weakness sometimes. I've felt it to be painful and calloused and bitter. Having a tough and strong appearance gave me something to hide behind. Not really strong, but defensive.

Even a lifelong attempt to become genuinely strong on our own is a weak pursuit. Ultimately, we cannot lift the hard, heavy stuff on our own. We cannot lift life and live life to move forward on our own. We cannot just become strong. We must learn to ask for help. Even when we hate asking for help, wanting to hold the pride of being 'strong' and being able to do it all 'on our own,' we can keep learning.

While we learn, we can begin to ask God to anoint us with the oil of joy because the joy of the LORD is our strength. We can also learn that if we want to walk in God's will for our life, He will ask us to do things we cannot do on our own, but by working with Him, it will work out. We really don't want to try to live life on our own, without God, do we? God is with us. God is for us. Do we believe it?

· · ● ● ● · ● ● ● · ·

13 I can do all this through him who gives me strength.

Philippians 4:13

19

The Sovereign Lord is my strength;

he makes my feet like the feet of a deer,

he enables me to tread on the heights.

For the director of music. On my stringed instruments.

Habakkuk 3:19

10 Nehemiah said, "Go and enjoy choice food and sweet drinks, and send some to those who have nothing prepared. This day is holy to our Lord. Do not grieve, for the joy of the Lord is your strength."

Nehemiah 8:10

Prayer

LORD, give me more strength when I cry these tears, when I want to scream, when I want to run away but should stay, when I want to stay but should get out, when I cower but should stand up straight, when I want to hide but should show my face, when I want to judge and convict people but should keep my mouth shut, when I should speak up against injustice or another wrong I witness but want to ignore it. LORD, I cannot do this life without You and I cannot accomplish anything without Your presence which brings such joy. Ignite my heart with Your flame and drench my spirit with the oil of joy. Make my spirit and presence electrified with Your joy anointing my heart. LORD, may my cup overflow with all the blessings of joy You've given me. May I be a strong woman because of all the joy You have given to strengthen me. In JESUS' name I ask You for this and believe I shall receive more joy to make me strong. I know You will answer my prayers because You give me strength to accomplish what You've called me to do. THANK YOU. AMEN.

Questions for Reflection

In what ways do you think you are strong? In what ways do other people think you are strong?

How have you witnessed God giving you strength through changing your attitude to be positive?

In what ways can you be seeking God's strength and joy? Make a list of at least 5 things that bring you joy. Thank God for these things and think about them when you need to be strong.

• • ● ● ● • ● ● • •

Writing Prompt

Write about a time you felt the strongest.

Notes

16

ON TEA

I love tea! Drinking it, smelling it, learning about it, looking at it. I love tea things, too: fragile china tea cups and saucers, tea spoons, the small plates where you set your tea bag, tea bags, the packets the tea comes in, boxes of tea, tins of tea, tea timers, tea cozies, tea kettles, tea pots, tea caddies, tea mugs, tea cakes, scones, muffins, cookies, biscuits, tiny triangular cucumber sandwiches with the crusts cut off, tea strainers, tea infusers, tea shops, iced tea, tapioca pearls, bobas, hot tea, tea lattes, oolong, green tea, black tea, herbal and fruit infusions, rooibus, yerba mate, jasmine.

My absolute favorite place to go for tea is not too far from where I grew up. My mom and I would go there often, and we have learned a lot about tea from the owners. One thing we've learned is there are certain time limits in which you must steep your tea. The longer the tea or tisane infuses or steeps, the stronger, more flavorful, or in some cases the more bitter it becomes. With herbal and fruit infusions, the longer you leave the bag in the water, the more flavor and intensity you'll get from it.

While being in God's presence can be enjoyable like with tea, God is unlike the teas. Over brewing some teas turns into a bitter drink. When we spend extended time brewing in God's presence, we become a better flavor. We can spend all our precious time steeping and dwelling in His presence and we will never become bitter, but we will become more and more fragrant as He fills us with His presence. We can be steeped, fraught with and overflowing with the Holy Spirit and His goodness. We can have the Holy Spirit coming out of our pores. We can breathe in and smell of Him, as the water does with all varieties of teas.

As people of God, we can easily bring people into God's presence when we are full of the Holy Spirit. When we waft a refreshing and comforting fragrance with each interaction, it can be transformative for us and others.

4 Remain in me, as I also remain in you. No branch can bear fruit by itself; it must remain in the vine. Neither can you bear fruit unless you remain in me.

John 15:4

Prayer

LORD, give me grace and patience to steep myself, as a tea or tisane, in Your presence, Word, and company, so I will mix permanently with the water of Your Spirit. May there be no distinguishing place of where You start and where I end, that You and I would be inseparable and irreversible once I've steeped in, dwelt in, You, just as a cup of tea can never turn into just water again. I never want to be my fleshly self again. I want You to transform me into a new and life-giving creation. Praise You for Your goodness! Thank You in Jesus' name. AMEN.

Questions for Reflection

What does your daily time with God normally look like?

How might you like to incorporate spending time dwelling in or steeping in the LORD's presence?

What are obstacles that prevent or make it difficult for you to simply brew in God's presence? Write these down, then give them up to God. Ask Him how you can get rid of these blocks.

• • ● ● ● • ● ● ● • •

Writing Prompt

Write about drinking tea.

Notes

17

ON THE PILL

There are many forms of contraceptives. While there are also many viewpoints on birth control, both for and against its usage, I do not want to persuade anyone either way or to instigate a heated discussion where you are frustrated and no longer want to read this book.

Instead, I simply want to point out a few observations: the prefix *contra* means 'against' (and since I studied Spanish for several years, too, I can confirm that *contra* said in a different accent also means 'against'). So contraceptives are things which are against or opposed to or opposite of: *-cept* is a root word meaning to conceive (or come up with, generate, create, start, realize). The birth control user wants to be in control of the birthing of something, or the prevention of childbirth.

God has high thoughts and high dreams He wants to put inside of us. God wants us to conceive a big, God-sized dream within our hearts. He has big plans of hope and goodness for us, and He wants us to carry these dreams the full term until they are ready to be birthed, realized, achieved.

What if we consider the impact of trying to be against God's plans for our lives? Or what if we are trying to control something which God has for us? Maybe we can realize it's a better choice to take no preventative or controlling measures against whatever lovingkindness God wants to do in our hearts and lives, and for those all around us.

• • • • • • • • • •

11 For I know the plans I have for you," declares the Lord, "plans to prosper you and not to harm you, plans to give you hope and a future.

Jeremiah 29:11

• • • ● ● • ● ● • • •

Prayer

LORD, thank You that You want the best for me and thank You that I can trust You. Please help me become aware of the dreams and plans and hopes You have for me so I can start to walk in those. I want to partner with You to do the most I can to glorify You in Your kingdom. Please reveal to me, let me know what I'm doing that's causing any blockages keeping me from realizing the goals You have for my life. I surrender control of my life to You, Father. Thank You for Your Son overcoming death on the cross so I can live, allowing You to be in control. Thank You for hearing my prayers and having the best in mind for me. In Jesus' name. AMEN.

• • • ● ● • ● ● • • •

Questions for Reflection

What spiritual contraceptive are you using?

Ask God what might be in your life that is preventing you from receiving the first seeds of the dream God has for you?

What dreams has God planted inside you to grow and come to full fruition? Ask God how you can nurture these dreams?

• • • ● ● • ● ● • • •

Writing Prompt

My biggest dream from the wildest part of my imagination is _____.

Notes

18

ON TREATS

For one of my birthdays when I was a teenager, my best friend got me a whole bunch of my favorite treat. I was thrilled. It was one of the best presents I have ever received! I ate loads of the treats, taking breaks for a few weeks or days here and there, to ensure I still savored it but after quite a while, I still had a few boxes left. Well, I was afraid it had expired and was really sad I hadn't eaten it all. But, because I didn't know if they were okay (and a couple of times growing up we'd had bug problems in our kitchen cupboard with ants), I threw the rest away.

I didn't think they'd be seen, but my best friend happened to come over and saw the remaining boxes of treats in the garbage. Our eyes met when this discovery was made and to this day, several years later, the thought of the memory of my friend's face seeing that I'd seemingly carelessly disregarded such a special gift for me—I have tears in my eyes just thinking about it. I felt our friendship changed after this moment.

Yes, it was 'just a treat', but truly it was more than that and I hate it; I wish I'd kept and eaten it all because it probably would have been fine even a little past the expiration date. Still, I have such a deep regret about not only missing out on the fullness of such an amazingly delicious and special gift, but also the deep hurt my friend's face showed me. I am so sorry about what I did and I wish I could take it back.

Now, if my friend and I experienced such hurt and deep regret over discarded boxes of treats, can you imagine how God must feel when He offers His hand to us and we tell him no? Or how about when He says no, but we say yes and do or think something other than what He has for us? Or what if He gives us a special talent or skill or dream and we never do anything with it, disregard it, or worse, throw it away saying we don't think we want it anymore?

Note: Since first writing this, I have been able to speak to my friend. My friend said there were no hard feelings, and actually, my friend had forgotten that moment. I received my friend's forgiveness and no longer have regret about this situation, rather I have a healthy fear of giving up good gifts that were given especially to me.

11 If you, then, though you are evil, know how to give good gifts to your children, how much more will your Father in heaven give good gifts to those who ask him!

Matthew 7:11

Prayer

LORD, I don't want to have regret because I've hurt You. I want to be able to joyfully receive whatever gift You have for me, whether I think I'll like it or use it or not. Help me to trust You, that You will give me exactly what I need and that all Your gifts are good for me. I know You have my best interests in mind, and I just don't want to regret missing out on any of the fullness You have for me. I want the good gifts You have for me! LORD, I confess the times I've not taken full advantage of the gifts You have given me. I thank You for the cross and receive Your forgiveness with thanksgiving in my heart. I love You, Jesus. You are my best friend, and I really do not want to give You heartache because of me. In Jesus' name. Thank You, LORD, for hearing my prayer. AMEN.

· • • ● ● • ● ● • • ·

Questions for Reflection

What are gifts you know God has given you? How have you used these gifts?

What are gifts you would like God to give you? How would you like to use them?

What gifts have you refused to receive or to use properly? Ask God to forgive you and to show you how you can use and be blessed by these gifts.

· • • ● ● • ● ● • • ·

Writing Prompt

Write about the best or worst gift you ever received.

Notes

19

ON FIRE

When I was pursuing my undergraduate degree, I became really good friends with one of my professors and his wife. Several times I looked after their house while they were away. In order to be safe and comfortable there, my professor taught me how to build a fire in their fireplace. He also taught me how to build a bonfire, how to stack logs, how to use a snow blower, how to grill a steak, how to feed the deer and the birds in the woods, and how to change the timer on the water heater in the house, among many other things. They were very good friends to me.

This is how I learned to build a fire in the fireplace. First of all, make sure the vent is open so the house does not fill up with smoke. Then, loosely crumple old newspapers into log shapes and lay them in the bottom of the hearth in a crisscross arrangement so the air, and thus the fire, will draw upward. Kindling, dry bits of bark and small twigs or wood chips should be added next, loosely arranged to preserve the teepee and chimney effect from the newspaper.

Finally, add a couple of logs, crosshatched and touching but with plenty of air flow and leaning toward the back, so the fire will not fall out and into the room. Once it is prepared like this, double-check that the vent is in the open position and light a match and carefully ignite as much of the newspaper as is possible. Gently blow to help ignite the kindling and then the logs.

I house sat often and one time while I stayed over I was out of the room for quite awhile, leaving after the fire had died down, only to return wishing for a fire again. I was able to restart the fire without any new matches; I was very proud of myself.

There is something about fires that is so attractive and enticing, isn't there? Sitting around a cozy fire indoors or sitting in the cold winter bundled up for New Year's Eve bonfires, people just grow quiet and stare into the beautiful, dangerous flames that snap and eat anything they touch. Fire is fascinatingly all-consuming.

I think the same goes for someone who has a strong and bright personality. People are drawn to the passion that person has. Through the years as I've been involved with church things, I've been very excited to get to know so many Christians who are super passionate about the LORD. Lots of cultures these days, if they've ever been considered Christian, seem to be shifting toward a 'Post-Christian' slant.

As Christians, we've got to be excited to share the good news—the gospel of Christ's crucifixion and resurrection—with everyone around us in this 'I'm over it' culture. We know something life changing we want to pass around to everyone we meet. When we see people like this who are 'on fire for the Lord,' we often want this maturity and passion for ourselves.

It can be sort of frustrating sometimes when we experience more and more of God's goodness because many of us who say we are 'Christians' are more lethargic, being good people without making an impact with fiery passion. It is increasingly clear to me that I need to, we need to, wake up, look alive—and feel alive, passionate, and on fire for the LORD!

Just like my professor taught me in building a fire in the fireplace, passion for God takes time and careful preparation. When we as Christians aren't passionate about our relationship with God, but content to be good people, this is sad. We are missing out. We miss out on this fiery passion God gives us for His name and grace that gives us life and second chances.

Note: Please do not take offense if you are someone who is already passionate and on fire for the LORD and doing kingdom work. I pray you'd be inspired to keep burning hope and God's love to share. But if you are not fired up, with a furnace of the Holy Spirit in your body that urges you forth in His name, doing all things for His glory, then I plead with you in Jesus' name to get stirred up and fan the flame in your heart that is from God's word. Please make a difference for Jesus! If you've experienced God's transformative love and acceptance, please share your reason for hope with everyone you can.

9

But if I say, "I will not mention his word

   or speak anymore in his name,"

his word is in my heart like a fire,

   a fire shut up in my bones.

I am weary of holding it in;

   indeed, I cannot.

Jeremiah 20:9

Prayer

LORD, wake up all the deadness and laziness in each of us so we can actually make a difference and enhance Your kingdom. I want the Church to be on fire with passionate love and urgency to proclaim Your love, who You are. Stir up in our hearts, LORD, a passion for Your name. Encourage us to be overflowing with Your word and Your spirit so that we can't help but have it spill out and spread like an uncontrollable forest fire. Teach us to keep the fire burning in a manner productive for Your kingdom. But LORD, if it is Your will, I pray You would ignite us as Your Bride to be passionately in love and zealous for You. I pray our passion and fire for You would be contagious and others would come to know and love You and be filled with Your same Holy Fiery Spirit. In Jesus' name, thank You. AMEN.

· · • ● ● · ● ● • ·

Questions for Reflection

How on fire for the LORD are you? On a scale from 1-5, rate yourself: 1 being wet ground, unable to ignite, and 5 being all ablaze, the heat impacting and warming others up to the idea of relationship and eternity with the LORD.

If you are not on fire, how can you open up for God to ignite you? If you are on fire for Him, how can your fire burn more strongly, brightly, warmly? Ask God for grace to be closer to Him.

How often do you pray for revival for your nation, your city, your church? I recommend you begin to pray for God to set fire to the hearts around you, and in you! Ask God to give you His heart for prayer.

• • • ● ● • ● ● • • •

Writing Prompt

Write about a time you were excited to share something with others.

Notes

20

ON THANK YOU NOTES

M y sister almost always writes a thank you note any time she or her kids have received a gift. Even if it is a couple sentences of thanks, a thank you card can make the giver feel special and loved when she takes a moment to remember them. I am not as faithful at writing these notes as my sister. I always try to say thank you to the person when I receive a gift, but only sometimes do I manage to actually write a note.

I've heard good etiquette says a bride and groom should write thank you notes to guests within a couple months of the wedding, but not immediately. There should be a long enough time to allow the favor or the gift to be almost forgotten, but not quite. Enough time to pass to say, "I still remember your generosity after all this time, and I'm still thankful for you and what you've done, but I haven't done a quick, slapdash, get-it-over-with-right-away approach" and it wasn't an "oh crap! I still haven't written a note yet"—years later, either!

Any time we say 'thank you' or express thankfulness in another way, we look back—even if it was just a moment ago—and we are reminded of something good about someone. Most of the time being genuinely thankful toward someone helps solidify the relationship or feelings you have about that person, especially if they are already close, like a friend or relative. We think about how they are thoughtful, always around to bless and offer support.

Being thankful toward God increases our faith in Him. When we sincerely thank God for our every breath, our friends, our health, our achievements, our breakthroughs, our trials, our gifts and talents and opportunities from Him, for His character and entirely spotless track record for faithfulness, unconditional love and loyalty in our lives... we understand more of the consistency of God's character and our relationship with Him, and our trust in Him improves and intensifies. When we are thankful, we notice the goodness.

• • • • ● • ● ● • •

6 Do not be anxious about anything, but in every situation, by prayer and petition, with thanksgiving, present your requests to God.

Philippians 4:6

• • • • ● • ● ● • •

Prayer

LORD, thank You. You are good. Thank You that nothing can separate us from Your love. Thank You that You—and only You, no matter what I say or do—are always in control. Thank You that You never change. Thank You for wavy hair. Thank You for beautiful early morning sunrises and late night sunsets. Thank You that You've laid out a path for me to take. Thank You for friends I get to watch chick flicks with. Thank You for my taste buds. Thank You for lemons and limes and for amazingly massive burritos with spicy salsa. Thank You that You never change. Thank You that You have a good plan for me to prosper and for me to be unharmed. Thank You for Your love. In Jesus' name. AMEN.

• • • • ● • ● ● • •

Questions for Reflection

What are you thankful for?

For whom are you thankful? Take a moment to write a note sharing why you are thankful for them.

How often do you thank God? I encourage you to take on a lifestyle of thanksgiving. I truly believe when we thank God, our faith increases with each thankful expression.

· • ● ● ● • ● ● ● • •

Writing Prompt

Write about a time when you felt overwhelmed with gratitude.

Notes

Scan here to grab a month of inspiring journal prompts to grow in your gratitude practice. My gift to you! Happy writing and happy gratitude-ing!

21

On Shampoo

When we installed a new shower head in our bath, showering was like standing beneath a gentle spring rain cloud. One day, my shower completely enveloped me, the water at its most perfect warmth cascading, the scent of my new chemical-free natural soap in all of its lavender relaxation, and luxury bubbling up around me. Then I squeezed some thick shampoo into my hand, wetted my hair and began the best part of the shower: Lather. Rinse. Repeat.

Whenever I get my hair cut, the part I most look forward to is the shampooing because of the head massage. I always feel sad when they finish because they just stroke and gently play with my hair, cleansing my scalp and mind of dirt and tension. Oh, it feels so good! Sometimes washing my own hair is lovely and other times, I just want to get it over with because I have other things I need to do. Lather. Rinse. Towel Dry. Run off onto the next thing. That mundane nature of having to wash to get clean can seem like so much sameness, so annoying.

Lather. Rinse. Repeat.

Prayer feels like this sometimes. But I've read the prayer of the righteous is effective. If our hearts are good with God's heart, He will happily do His will, knowing our hearts want Him to do His will for our lives. God doesn't get sick of hearing our voices praying to Him. He wants us to lather, to be in His presence for lots of time, really soaking up all of His cleansing goodness. Then He wants us to rinse the hair of our lives to get rid of all the dirt and gunk and the worry of letting go...and then, He wants us to repeat the whole process again and again and again. He never gets bored being with us. He is more interested in the sameness of our prayers than little kids are in their own repetition of activities.

There is a story about when Jesus tells the tired fishermen to throw out their nets again despite having only just brought everything in and docked up at the end of an unproductive day. They had completed their mundane task: "lathering" in the boat fishing, doing their job. Then, they "rinsed" themselves from their livelihood and closed up shop for the day. Well, nearly closed up.

Jesus, He is God, and so often He has a different and better idea. He doesn't get bored with anything we do that is a bunch of sameness. It's all about relationship with Him. He wants to hear our voice and He wants us to cast out our nets to try again. And He wants us to give Him all of our lives, surrendering again and again. He loves us and cares about us no matter how we feel about the everyday same old, same old.

7 Cast all your anxiety on him because he cares for you.

1 Peter 5:7

Prayer

LORD, You are my God, and I am so grateful You desire my company and You think I am someone worthwhile. Thank You that You never get tired of hearing my prayers and requests. LORD, I really don't want to grow tired of coming to You, either. I want to be with You and I want to trust You with all of the things in my life, even when it means I need to continually try again and ask You to meet with me again and again. Thank You for Your grace to let me come to You, LORD. AMEN.

· • ● ● ● • ● ● • • ·

Questions for Reflection

What is something you have been asking God for help with time and again? Take a moment right now to bring it before the LORD again. Yes, ask Him again.

What do you think some benefits are of lathering, rinsing, and repeating the whole process with God?

Remember a time God told you to throw out your nets again after you had just cleaned up. How did that go for you? Ask God to show you what He's doing in this situation.

· • ● ● ● • ● ● • • ·

Writing Prompt

Write about taking a shower.

Notes

22

On My Two Front Teeth

Around Christmas there is a silly song all of us can relate to. A kid sings about wanting his adult teeth to grow in. It's a cute song, but do you also remember when you lost your front teeth? Life was much easier. What is on your wishlist? Toys, games, gadgets, clothes, books, movies, gift cards?

One of the best presents I received one year when I was about six was a gigantic Barbie® Fold 'N Fun House. It was a luggage box or tote-sized thing that folded out into an amazing house that even had a patio and a mailbox with a street light you could turn on with a switch—batteries not included. My Fitness Fun Barbie® with moveable joints for active exercise poses was another favorite—she enjoyed her big house.

Maybe you are like the little kid in the song and you have no interest in all of these material things because you feel you have a big gap between the teeth of your life. When we feel the gap, what if the best gift for us is what David wants in the Psalms? The one thing David says he wants, above everything, is to see God's beauty and to dwell with Him.

• • • ● ● • ● ● • • •

One thing I ask from the Lord,

this only do I seek:

that I may dwell in the house of the Lord

all the days of my life,

to gaze on the beauty of the Lord

and to seek him in his temple.

Psalm 27:4

Prayer

LORD, change my heart, values, and priorities so my heart's cry can be the same as David's. Give me faithful eyes that focus entirely on You. LORD, make the big things bigger and the small things smaller so You get bigger to me and all of life's distractions get smaller. Show me Your beauty. God, I want to dwell in Your presence and live in Your house forever. Help me find favor so I can be with You. I want a supernatural gift of grace, please, so I can set aside everything but You. LORD, I want my heart to be transformed into such dependency on You that my only desire is to be with You, Jesus. I love You. In Your name. AMEN.

· · · · ● · ● ● · · ·

Questions for Reflection

What one thing do you desire more than anything? How do you do life with God as your central focus?

What steps can you take to make God, the one thing, the single most important thing in your life? Ask God for inspiration.

How will you gaze upon the LORD's beauty? How will you dwell in His house for all of your life? Ask God to show you how to connect and get closer to Him this season.

· · · · ● · ● ● · · ·

Writing Prompt

Write about beauty and your connection to it.

Notes

23

ON BOILING WATER

You know the saying, "A watched pot never boils." Technically, even if you watch a pot as it is in its boiling cycle, and it seems like it won't boil...eventually...after several minutes, it does! Try actually watching a pot boil. I'm serious. Fill up a nice pot with enough water that you would be able to use for dinner later to make pasta—I am not telling you to waste water and energy! Turn on the heat on your stove beneath the pot. Then pull up a chair and stare. If you actually do it, this point will hit home even more tangibly.

Even if you don't do this, I bet you are thinking, what a foolish idea! What a waste of time! I would never sit and watch a pot boiling, especially when I know it is going to work out and the cold water will become boiled water.

Pause a moment. Why then, do we sit and stare at situations in our lives we know are going to take awhile to work out? Think about the last time you said to God, I trust You and I am leaving this in Your hands. I know You are going to call me and let me know when everything is all set, so I am going to walk away, knowing You have the end result under control.

Sometimes we ask for things, and then when we finally get it, we are not quite sure of how to use it or what to do next. We can ask for wisdom during this time about how to use the gift once we have actually received it. We can work on this, to boldly approach God again and again about the same thing, and different things, too. We don't have to worry that He has forgotten. He remembers even when we struggle with leaving things alone.

If we can say with certainty we have poured our watery prayers into Jesus' pot, turned on the heat by submitting to His control—and walked away from the stove of life, then this is amazing. So many people struggle with letting go and trusting God. So, well done!

Now, there is absolutely nothing wrong with us continually asking God for the answers to our prayers, and actually this continued communication can strengthen our relationship with God—but we do not need to keep going over to the stove and checking on the water.

With water, we know it will eventually boil, and with prayer and God, we need to embrace this same knowledge and understanding of heat and thermal dynamics. We can keep asking Chef God if dinner's ready yet, and He can keep saying not yet, or we can be thankful our situation is in more than capable hands. Accepting this, we can then turn our attentions to something else while we wait for the water to boil—like what kind of pasta to have for dinner.

7 "Ask and it will be given to you; seek and you will find; knock and the door will be opened to you. **8** For everyone who asks receives; the one who seeks finds; and to the one who knocks, the door will be opened.

Matthew 7: 7-8

Prayer

Thank You Father that You know what is going on and You have it all under control. Thank You for being so trustworthy. Bless our relationship, so I can know You more to be sure You are as faithful as the claims in the Bible say. Increase my faith so I don't doubt Your word to take care of me and everything else. I want to fully trust You, and I lay my life down in Your hands. Let Your will be done. In Jesus' name. Let it be so. AMEN.

• • • ● ● • ● ● • • •

Questions for Reflection

What is something you've been waiting for that seems like you've been waiting for ages?

How is God telling you to respond?

What can you do to glorify God in the meantime while you are waiting? Ask God for ideas to connect with Him while you wait.

• • ● ● ● • ● ● • • •

Writing Prompt

Write about a time in childhood when all your waiting was worth it.

Notes

24

ON THE MAN IN THE RED JACKET

When I was an undergraduate, I was part of a Christian campus ministry. One year, I went with them on a missions trip to Chicago, Illinois. We went into areas in Chicago where the Projects were and where the city was housing low income folks. We were told the city was displacing these people by knocking down the apartment buildings in the Projects and "cleaning up" the neighborhood.

One day my group met a man who was wearing a red jacket. He talked to us and told us a story about himself. He said he met Jesus, but didn't feel like he could get out of his situation. He was a security guard for the drug dealers who yelled profanity at us "white people." We prayed for him, but quickly got out of there when things got heated and we were made very unwelcome. As we went away, the man in the red jacket called after us, "Remember me!" and I have.

There's a song I remember about going through a hard time, but how they were able to make it through. They believed someone had been praying for them and that's why it all worked out. We certainly do not always get to see the results of our prayers, but we can actually be sure our prayers make a difference in people's lives.

There are many seemingly crazy stories about people who have survived horrible disasters, only to find out their family members or friends were awoken, perhaps at random, in the middle of the night to pray for them without knowing why. Let's not ignore a prompting to pray for someone. Who knows what our prayers could do for them?

• • • ● ● • ● ● • •

18 And pray in the Spirit on all occasions with all kinds of prayers and requests. With this in mind, be alert and always keep on praying for all the Lord's people.

Ephesians 6:18

3 And pray for us, too, that God may open a door for our message, so that we may proclaim the mystery of Christ, for which I am in chains.

Colossians 4:3

• • • ● ● • ● ● • •

Prayer

Dear God, teach me to listen and be alert to Your promptings. Teach me to hear Your voice and help me have grace to respond accordingly. When I pray, I don't want my words to just go out (and on and on) just for the sake of saying something, but I want to pray with purpose. Put people on my heart to pray for. Give me wisdom and knowledge about how to pray for them. Then, LORD, hear my prayers and answer them as quickly as is Your will to do. I pray, too, that You'd continue to prompt people to pray for me as well. I'd love to be able to share stories of my own about how I could tell someone must've been praying for me. I want to encourage others to keep praying and keep remembering to pray for people they know and even those they don't know. Change my heart to be filled with prayers. Thank You, LORD. In Your name. AMEN.

· · · ● ● · ● ● · · ·

Questions for Reflection

Do you know someone whose memory has been calling out to you? Please listen and please pray for them. Ask God for guidance on how to pray for them.

Who do you pray for on a regular basis? If you don't regularly pray, make a list of 3-5 friends or family members. Keep it simple, but be faithful to pray every day or once a week, but be consistent to support them with prayer.

How often do you pray for people you don't know? What benefit might there be to pray for your neighborhood? City and county officials? National leaders? Persecuted Christians? Missionaries? Human trafficking victims and their traffickers? Starving and uneducated people in the Third World? Pick someone or some people group to pray for. Your prayers do make a difference.

· · · ● · ● · ● ● · · ·

Writing Prompt

Write about your personal experience with suffering an injustice.

Notes

25

ON LIGHTNING BOLTS AND LIMOUSINES

When I was little, about 5 or 6 years old, I had solid plans for my future adult life. I wanted a hot pink jeep. My house was going to be black with neon green and neon yellow lightning bolts. Here was my biggest plan for my life: I would have a stretch limousine, also with neon lightning bolts painted on the outside, but on the inside, there would be a large hot tub in the back for me and a long conveyor belt the whole length of the limo, so my husband could send me drinks when I was in the back in the hot tub. This was going to work so well because while he would be driving, he'd still be able to serve me!

Surprisingly, my tastes have altered slightly since then, but I marvel at my own childish imagination. I still have quite a vivid imagination and most mornings I wake up saying, "I had the weirdest dream last night!" I am also conscious of what visual images my eyes perceive. I don't do well with horror films. I always say, "I don't need help with my imagination!"

Have you ever tried to control your imagination, tried to keep it from getting carried away? Have you kept your creativity harnessed and under wraps? Have you been scolded for your outlandish thoughts as a child? Did your parents, or others you admired as a young person, shoot you down by saying you were aiming too high or thinking too ambitiously? Who have you now discouraged from blossoming in their creativity? Have you placed this negative hindering criticism upon a young mind?

Uh-oh...

We were created in the image of God. The fact that we follow and look to a creator—the Creator of everything we can see and experience and more means that since we are made in His image, we are meant to be creative, too. Double uh-oh...so, that means whenever we put down our own creativity or another's, we are saying "No" to God and His creative will for us.

We see in the beginning God gave Adam the joyful job—without toil!—to use his creative juices to name every living thing the saw. God blessed Adam as he operated in his gifting and natural abilities, which were given to him directly by God! Being creative is not an option for our life with God, it is a command. When we allow ourselves to do God's creative will in our lives and operate in those creative expressions, we also encourage all those around us to do the same.

19 Now the Lord God had formed out of the ground all the wild animals and all the birds in the sky. He brought them to the man to see what he would name them; and whatever the man called each living creature, that was its name.

Genesis 2:19

Prayer

Father God, thank You for creating me in Your image. I'm so glad I can be creative, that I have your permission and actually Your command to do so. I want to make and do stuff that is creative because I want all You have for me. I want to do Your will. I pray ideas would never stop coming to my mind. Increase my desire for learning and increase my capacity for doing new things. Take all my time and efforts and products of my being obedient in creating as worship to You. In Jesus' artistic name. AMEN.

• • • • ● • ● • • •

Questions for Reflection

What do you enjoy doing? Brainstorm a list of things you like to make or do that require even the slightest amount of creativity (e.g., making a meal, planning an event, choosing a color and painting a room, writing poetry, building a treehouse, etc.).

How can you adjust your mindset to embrace being obedient in creating something, and then knowing you are actually worshipping God? Ask God to give you the perspective to see the impact you have as you create.

What are a couple things you have wanted to learn how to do (e.g., drawing, photography, computer stuff, a craft, changing fluids in your car, etc.)? Decide on one to learn first and do something to begin learning that thing: ask an expert, check out a book from the library, sign up for a class. God wants you to be creative, to be yourself. When you are obedient, you honor and bless him.

Who else can you encourage to work on doing creative things, too? Arrange to talk with them about it.

• • • ● ● • ● ● • •

Writing Prompt

Write about childhood dreams.

Notes

26

ON CALLING AUTOMATED PHONE LINES

During my early days living in England, I had the cheapest little Nokia phone with a tiny, pixelated screen that wasn't suitable for online browsing–it was definitely not a smart phone. I wasn't sure how long I'd be in England, so I didn't want a long contract that I was stuck with, so I just had a "top up" option where I could add credit when I needed it.

One night I really wanted to use the credit already on my mobile phone to do a top up (add more calling and texting credit), so I could use my credit effectively. So, I called Customer Service and got the automated system my mobile phone carrier has put into place. I called a couple of times, in fact, and I could not figure out how I'd done this before. There were so many options and I was beyond confused. I just wanted to talk to a person.

There are some automated phone systems I do really like, such as 24-hour library book renewal. Often I still forget until after the due date to renew them, but at least, then, I won't have a library person scolding me for my overdue behavior. It's also really nice to not have to go to the library just to renew the books.

Another nice automated system is when you have to call your credit card company to notify them of travel plans. You just have to answer one of a few secret questions (that you had set up, so you should know the answers to them), your address, your credit card number and your travel dates. I am sure there have been times when you have wished you could just quickly call somewhere, but had to go through a lengthy process of speaking to seemingly incompetent and bored call center employees and being put on hold several times, forced to listen to that snappy 30-second clip of hold music.

And possibly, you have experienced my 'top up experience' when I needed more than a dozen menus each with 3-5 options, and then pushing star to repeat, and the hash, or pound, key to exit the current m enu...How exhausting! When we want to talk to God, it's not complicated. We don't need a number for His direct line. There is no holding, no menus, no transfers. We can talk to God right now.

3 'Call to me and I will answer you and tell you great and unsearchable things you do not know.'

Jeremiah 33:3

Prayer

God, thanks so much that You are so amazing that You want a personal relationship with me. Thank You for Jesus conquering death on the cross so there would no longer be any separation between us, so now I do, by Your grace, have a direct line to You. And thank You that You desire and encourage and expect me to be in constant use of my direct line to You. Thank You that You want to hear from me about anything and everything. Thank You that You respond! You are so good. Increase my ability to hear Your voice because I want to take in all of the amazing things You have to say to me. In Jesus' name. AMEN.

Questions for Reflection

When you die and go to heaven, what questions would you like to ask God? Ask him now and wait for a response.

What do you want to say to Him? Say it right now. He's listening and hearing your voice. He wants a relationship with you, so He's dying (He's already died) to be able to hear directly from you.

How often do you call or text your friends or family during the week? How about God? What needs to change so you make time to talk to God more often? Ask God to reveal to you how you can connect with him more.

• • • ● ● • ● ● • • •

Writing Prompt

Write about your most memorable customer service experience.

Notes

27

ON ANTS

M y first home in England was in a highly populated area: student central. Every day I would sit at my kitchen table and look out into the park. Every day I would watch hundreds, if not thousands, of university students amble along to class, though some with more speed than others when the top of the hour was near.

There are about 5 kilometers (3.5 miles) of walking paths throughout the park and around the perimeter. All paths lead to a central point in the park, which then breaks off into separate directions on the other side. Knowing this as I stared out into the park, I couldn't help but think these students are worker ants who are all making the long, strenuous trek back to the ant hill.

When I was little, I did not (and still don't) like bugs. I'd sweep them off my driveway at home, ridding it of anthills. Then, I would watch in amazement, and slight annoyance, at the speed with which the mound would be rebuilt by these same ants! For being blind and small, they sure quickly figure out what needs to get done. Each one naturally, almost immediately, picks up its fixing equipment so the preliminary hills get recreated in a matter of seconds.

Seeing these students, the future leaders of our world, makes me wonder what would happen if people did life like the ants. There is a need in our world. What if we all dropped what we were doing to attend to the need...in Jesus' name? We aren't necessarily doing the wrong things in life, but perhaps we could reexamine our hearts and motives for why we are doing whatever we're doing. If we are doing something because of its benefits to ourselves, we may have room for improvement. If, however, we are doing something that more directly serves people for God, it's likely a bigger benefit to the kingdom.

There are so many needs all around us. It can be as simple as helping an old lady cross the street safely or having a half hour coffee chat with a neighbor or a new mom. It could also be a more complex team effort like landscaping someone's garden, picking up litter in the city, or organizing a community outreach program.

The sky is the limit. And really, with God, what we think of as impossible is possible with God. Even if a particular thing is done by an individual for God, lots of individuals together have an even bigger impact. We can be a team for the LORD even if we aren't directly involved with each other.

· · ● ● ● · ● ● · ·

8

He has shown you, O mortal, what is good.

And what does the Lord require of you?

To act justly and to love mercy

and to walk humbly[a] with your God.

Micah 6:8

• • • ● ●• ● ● • • •

Prayer

God, I'm thankful for all the wonderful opportunities You put in my path. I hope and pray I notice. I want to be as much of a blessing as I can in Your name. Help me see You and others at work, so I can join in with what is already happening and so Your will can be done on earth as it is in heaven. Raise up leaders who desire to help those who need it. Help me to notice those who need You and give me courage to meet them where they are. Help me actually help them, so I can be a welcome light to them in their dark place. LORD, fill me up to overflowing with Your Spirit and Your love so I can't help but pour out Your lovingkindness onto them. Be glorified in Jesus' name. AMEN.

• • • ● ●• ● ● • • •

Questions for Reflection

How are you currently serving God and serving people? Would you like to be doing something else instead of or in addition to this? If so, what?

How well do you know your neighbors? What can you do this week, or even today, that is a real practical way of serving? Ask God to highlight someone to reach out to today. It might be as simple as introducing yourself and learning their name.

What is God calling you to do alongside a group of Jesus followers? If you don't know what needs there are, spend a couple minutes asking God to show you.

· • ● ● ● • ● ● • ·

Writing Prompt

Write about an injustice or a disparity you're passionate about helping to improve.

Notes

28

On Rascal

R ascal sells magazines to tourists and other shoppers of the downtown area. People like Rascal are bound by addiction and bad circumstances. Lying and deceit, driven by any addiction, is usually what grips their entire being. Sometimes he wanders the streets away from the city and tries to panhandle his stories of misfortune and tells those who give him a penny that they have somehow restored his faith in humanity.

The irony in this situation is that Rascal tells this same elaborate story of lies without being conscious of telling lies or doing anything wrong. These lies have become his way of life. For any of us who help, and know the reality of Rascal's story, we actually may need our faith in humanity to be restored. Or maybe we just need our faith in God amplified.

Sometimes I think we can get lost in a story of our own misfortune—we fabricate this tale to get pity from friends, relatives, strangers, ourselves—or even God. But God knows our hearts and He knows Rascal's heart. No matter what we hide from God, intentionally or not, God knows our thoughts from far away (Psalm 139:2) and there is no place we can go to get away from His presence (Psalm 139:7).

God undoubtedly knows exactly what we are up to at any point in time and He is always around us whether we acknowledge Him or not. So let's stop trying to leave Him. He already knows what's up and wants to help us more than we want to help ourselves. Will we allow God into our lives in this moment so together we can turn our lives around to be closer to God and really know Him?

Note: Rascal is not one specific person, but a mixture of people who I have met and seen in the city and those about whom I have heard stories from other people who have also reached out to help those on the street.

3

You discern my going out and my lying down;

　you are familiar with all my ways.

4

Before a word is on my tongue

　you, Lord, know it completely.

Psalm 139: 3-4

Prayer

Dear LORD, thank You that You know what I'm up to and nothing I can do will ever surprise You. You know my ways and You know my heart and thoughts better than I know these things about myself. Help me see what's offensive to You so we can get rid of it and turn around to walk in the way of everlasting life with You. Change my heart and mind, Oh God. Thank You for knowing me so well. Help me know You better, so I will have the opportunity to grow closer to You. I want to know You as well as You know me! I love You, LORD, in Jesus' name. AMEN.

• • • ● ● • ● ● • • •

Questions for Reflection

What kind of thought life do you have? How would you feel if your thoughts were played on a screen to an audience of friends and family?

What might you be trying to hide from God? Ask God for grace to not hide anymore.

How might you declare that you follow Jesus? How might you share your shortcomings and sins? How might you praise God in this moment? If you're unsure of your next step, ask God to guide you in what to do.

• • • ● ● • ● ● • • •

Writing Prompt

Write about a lie.

Notes

29

On the Whistling Man

When I first lived in England, nearly every day at some point around midday, I could expect to hear a few moments of clear blue whistling. I would always run to the window, sometimes jumping up onto the counter and leaning out the window to see if I could see the whistling person.

It always brought me such joy to hear it. Even now, the memory of the whistling is comforting to me. From other people in the area, I learned the whistler is an older man who always walks his dog in the park. These other people had already seen him, but I hadn't. They said they found him amusing, but would shrug their shoulders at my own amazement at their having witnessed the source of whistling. I asked them not to tell me any details about their encounters with the whistling man because I wanted to fully experience it myself.

With this incredible amount of mystery and intrigue in this unknown for me, I almost didn't want to see the whistling man. I enjoyed this pursuit and expectation, this running to the window to open it to catch an ear-filled glimpse of only what my ears could see. Do you have some mystery like this that fascinates you? The reality for me is that it's just a guy who whistles.

What if we pursued God with this intrigue, anticipation, curiosity and fervor? What if God is teaching us about His graceful mystery as we desire to discover our own fascinating, mysterious whistling man?

Part of the mystery is musical. Music is a gift from God, too. He sings and dances over us, not just in our neighborhood, but directly over us. He takes pleasure in us, so let's celebrate!

• • • ● ● • ● ● ● • •

17

The Lord your God is with you,

the Mighty Warrior who saves.

He will take great delight in you;

in his love he will no longer rebuke you,

but will rejoice over you with singing."

Zephaniah 3:17

• • • ● ● • ● ● ● • •

Prayer

LORD, I want to see You with all my heart, soul, mind, and strength. I want a hunger and desire and eagerness to meet with You just like I have in meeting with other exciting things, but I want to have more excitement about getting to be with You, my LORD, my Savior, my Friend, Lover, Father, and King. I know You love it when I seek You and I know You are beyond gladness with the love You have for me. Open my eyes and heart to perceive Your love for me and to grasp your picture of who I am to You and in You. Thank You that You are so pleased with me that You sing and dance. In Jesus' name. Thank You, LORD, for Your love. AMEN.

• • • ● • ● ● • • •

Questions for Reflection

How would you describe your level of excitement to meet with and spend time with God?

How does this level of excitement compare with another favorite activity of yours?

What qualities do you possess that people can perceive to know your excitement? How can you transfer these traits onto time spent with God?

What does the verse, Zephaniah 3:17, mean to you? How do you think God rejoices over you with singing? Ask God to show you what it's like to have Him celebrate you.

· · ● ● ● · ● ● ● · ·

Writing Prompt

Write about a childhood celebration.

Notes

30

ON BABY WASHCLOTHS

When I was a teenager, I began crocheting and knitting. Eventually, I picked up a couple how-to knitting books with patterns and detailed instructions. They helped me to complete my first ever pair of socks and kid-sized sweaters. It's all very exciting. These socks and cardigans are really complicated, though. At one point in my early knitting days, many people around me were about to have babies. I thought it'd be fun to give them something, but as the aunt to several little ones, I understand how much junk is accumulated. It can be so expensive.

I decided with a shaky deep breath I would try something new. I would knit baby washcloths. I had never done this before: which pattern, yarn, color, needles, size should I choose? I asked my knitting expert mother-in-law for help. Once I chose all the details, I started to knit. I followed the pattern, tried not to regret doing a new thing. Eventually, I got a complete set of rows finished to fully see the design—easy! Looking back now, it all makes sense—the pattern maker knew what she was doing despite my uncertainty.

When God, the creator of the universe (a.k.a. Ultimate Pattern Maker) says something like knit two, purl three, etc., pertaining to our situation, we can follow Him. We can be confident He knows what is going on, and when we look back at our "baby washcloth" life we'll see the design coming into form and then we'll want to follow Him more.

As with knitting, we do need to understand the big picture, the end product, but sometimes it just gets too confusing. Taking a step back and simply knitting, living, one row at a time often allows things to fall into place. Sometimes God gives us just one row at a time, illuminating just what we need to know before moving on, and He asks us to trust Him to show the way, having given us a great instruction manual—not for knitting, but for life—the Bible.

105

Your word is a lamp for my feet,

a light on my path.

Psalm 119:105

Prayer

Lord, give me a hunger for Your Word. Thank You for how it leads and guides me along the way. Help me to turn to You, the Word, and the Bible, the Word you've given me, to know how to live my life. Help me to be content to lean on Your Word to have it as the illustration for me to move forward. Thank You for guiding me. I want to follow You in Jesus' name. AMEN.

Questions for Reflection

How often do you spend time reading the Bible and learning from it? If you are unsure about what to read, consider getting a Bible that is set up to read or study in one year.

What does typical time spent reading the word look like for you? What do you wish it could be like?

What do you struggle with or want more of when you read the Bible? Ask God right now to help you with that particular area.

• • • ● • ● ● • • •

Writing Prompt

Write about the process of learning a new thing which is now part of your everyday life.

Notes

T hank you so much for reading my book! What did you think?

I really appreciate all of your feedback and I love hearing what you have to say.

Here's the thing: I need your input to make my future books even better.

Please take two minutes now to leave a helpful review online to let me know what you thought of the book.

Scan this code to bring you to the review site.

Thanks so much! :)

Happy writing!

Molly

INDEX: Verses

Jeremiah 29:11 On The Pill (17)

Jeremiah 33:3 On Calling Automated Phone Lines (26)

Micah 6:8 On Ants (27)

Habakkuk 3:19 On Weightlifting (15)

Zephaniah 3:17 On the Whistling Man (29)

· • ● ● ● • ● ● ● • ·

New Testament

Matthew 7: 7-8 On Boiling Water (23)

Matthew 7:11 On Treats (18)

Mathew 9:37-38 On Gardening (5)

Matthew 28:19 On Dreaming (1)

John 15:4 On Tea (16)

Romans 8:14-17 On Fathers (2)

Ephesians 6:18 On the Man in the Red Jacket (24)

Philippians 3:12-14 On the Mile Run (13)

Philippians 4:6 On Thank You Notes (20)

Philippians 4:13 On Weightlifting (15)

Colossians 4:3 On the Man in the Red Jacket (24)

James 1:2-4 On Mud (14)

James 3:17 On Pomegranates (3)

1 Peter 2:12 On Broccoli Sunshine (11)

1 Peter 5:7 On Shampoo (21)

2 Peter 3:8 On Timers (7)

• • • ● ● • ● ● • •

Note: I've included stories about real people who are friends and family of mine and I have, to the best of my ability, contacted them to obtain permission to tell their story to help encourage you in this book. Where it's not been possible, I've altered names and circumstances.

About the Author

M olly Ann Ovenden is a British American originally from Minnesota. From 2010 to 2017, she lived in West Yorkshire, England, with her bearded furniture-making Englishman husband, Max. They moved to Northern Minnesota in 2017.

Molly is a creative writing coach who helps people become the writers they've dreamed of being through courses, community and coaching.

When she's not writing or coaching, she's reading, laughing, smiling, eating, drinking tea and coffee, painting, daydreaming, training for a marathon, doing yoga, or going for circular walks.

She hopes and prays you really love this book and share it with all of your friends.

CPSIA information can be obtained
at www.ICGtesting.com
Printed in the USA
LVHW050215220523
747655LV00011B/707

9 798986 053400